Developing *literacy* Skills

Through Geography

KEY STAGE 2: Y5-6
P6-7

FRANCES MACKAY

HOPSCOTCH
EDUCATIONAL PUBLISHING

Contents

Published by Hopscotch Educational Publishing Ltd, 29 Waterloo Place, Leamington Spa CV32 5LA. (Tel: 01926 744227)

© 2001 Hopscotch Educational Publishing

Written by Frances Mackay
Series design by Blade Communications
Illustrated by Jane Bottomley
Cover illustrated by Susan Hutchison
Printed by Clintplan, Southam

Frances Mackay hereby asserts her moral right to be identified as the author of this work in accordance with the Copyright, Designs and Patents Act, 1988.

ISBN 1-902239-80-6

Introduction

✦ ABOUT THE SERIES ✦

Developing Literacy Skills Through Geography is a series of books aimed at developing key literacy skills using a range of written genres based on a geography theme, from Key Stage 1 through to Key Stage 2. The series offers a structured approach which provides detailed lesson plans to teach specific literacy and geographical skills. A unique feature of the series is the provision of differentiated photocopiable activities aimed at considerably reducing teacher preparation time. Suggestions for follow-up activities for both literacy and geography ensure maximum use of this resource.

✦ ABOUT THIS BOOK ✦

This book is for teachers of children at Key Stage 2, Years 5–6. It aims to:

✦ develop children's literacy and geography skills through exposure to and experience of a wide range of stimulating texts with supporting differentiated activities which are both diversified and challenging;

✦ support teachers by providing practical teaching methods based on whole-class, group, paired and individual teaching;

✦ encourage enjoyment and curiosity as well as develop skills of interpretation and response.

✦ CHAPTER CONTENT ✦

✦ Literacy objectives

This outlines the aims for the literacy activities suggested in the lesson plan.

✦ Geography objectives

This outlines the geography learning objectives that relate to the lesson plan.

✦ Resources

This lists the different resources that the teacher needs to teach the lesson.

✦ Starting point: Whole class

This provides ideas for introducing the activity and may include key questions to ask the children.

✦ Using the photocopiable text

This explains how to use the text extract provided with the children as a shared reading activity and introduction to the group work. It may also be used by groups during the group work.

✦ Group activities

This explains how to use each sheet as well as providing guidance on the type of child who will benefit most from each sheet.

✦ Plenary session

This suggests ideas for whole-class sessions to discuss the learning outcomes and follow-up work.

✦ Follow-up ideas for literacy

This contains suggestions for further literacy activities related to the lesson plan which can be carried out at another time.

✦ Follow-up ideas for geography

This contains suggestions for further geography activities related to the lesson plan which can be carried out at another time.

In the news – 1

 ## Literacy objectives

- ✦ To understand dramatic conventions, including:
  - the conventions of scripting
  - how character can be communicated in words and gestures
  - how tension can be built up through pace, silences and delivery.

  (Y5: T1, T5)
- ✦ To write own play script. (Y5: T1, T18)

 ## Geography objectives

(Unit 16)
- ✦ To understand how people affect the environment.
- ✦ To show how different people might respond to a change in their local area.

 ## Resources

- ✦ If possible, some local or national newspaper reports about disputes, such as building new supermarkets or houses on greenfield sites.

 ## Starting point: Whole class

- ✦ Tell the children that they are going to read a play script about a dispute between the people of a village and a developer who wants to build a supermarket nearby.
- ✦ Are the children aware of any similar disputes in their own local area? If so, discuss the outcomes of the plans and what the local people thought/did. If this is not relevant, share some information about an issue in another area (either by reading out some newspaper reports or by telling the children yourself).
- ✦ Talk about how there are always two sides to a dispute and that people will have very different reasons why they might be for or against a new project. Relate this to the children's own area. What would they think if a developer wanted to pull down their playground, for example, and build houses on it? How would this affect them? What might they be able to do to stop it happening?
- ✦ Tell them that they will now read the play script to find out how a new plan can affect people in different ways.

 ## Using the photocopiable text

- ✦ Enlarge the text on page 6 or arrange for each pair of children to have a copy.
- ✦ Share the text. How can we tell it is a play script? What is different in the layout compared with a story, for example? Discuss how 'stage directions' are given and how we know how each character is speaking. What type of people do they think Mrs Jackson and Mrs Parsonage are? (Nosey? Like to gossip?) What clues in the text tell them this? (Is this why they are standing apart from the crowd?) What do they think of Norah? How are we made aware of people's feelings about the supermarket plans?
- ✦ Read through the script again, this time giving the children the different roles. What do they think might happen next? Discuss the possibilities – perhaps someone calms Peter and Bob down before they go into the meeting or perhaps the arrival of the developers stops their argument. What might happen at the meeting? What might the developers say to try and persuade the villagers to agree to the supermarket? What might some of the residents say in return? Write some of the children's ideas on the board.
- ✦ Tell the children that they are now going to finish the play script using these or their own ideas. Remind them of the conventions they need to use to finish it and how they should keep the conversations short to move the story on. Talk especially about how to end the script. Explain that the script does not need to continue for pages and pages! Ask them to think of a dramatic ending to conclude the meeting at the hall.

 ## Group activities

Using the differentiated activity sheets

Activity sheet 1: This sheet is aimed at children who need a lot of support in writing a play script. They are required to complete several lines of a given script.

Activity sheet 2: This sheet is aimed at children who are a little more confident in writing a script. They are given the same structure as on Activity sheet 1 but are required to complete more lines and directions.

In the news – 1

Activity sheet 3: This sheet is for more able children. They are required to write their own script with only the narrator's part as a guide.

 Plenary session

Share the responses to the activity sheets. How did the characters in the scripts respond to the meeting? Do the children think this might be how people in their local area would respond to the issue? Why/why not? How many different ways did the scripts end? How were the children able to show the tension or response to this ending in their script writing?

 Follow-up ideas for literacy

♦ Ask the children to pretend they are local reporters at the meeting. They could write an article for the newspaper about what happened at the meeting and the possible outcome.

♦ Use the script to explore idiomatic phrases, clichés and expressions. How could we alter the script to make more use of such phrases? Perhaps Mrs Jackson could use sayings such as 'I hope we're not being taken for a ride,', 'That Mr Page is well past his prime,' and so on.

♦ The children could create some posters – for and against the new supermarket. What arguments would they present? How might they convince others of their point of view?

♦ Challenge the children to write a set of comical instructions, such as 'How to upset everyone at a meeting' or 'How to make a supermarket developer disappear!'

♦ Act out the children's completed play scripts in groups. Ask the others to evaluate the script and the performance for their dramatic interest and impact. How could they be improved?

 Follow-up ideas for geography

♦ Ask the children to keep an eye out for newspaper stories about local changes. Make a class collection of them. Ask the children to write their own newspaper report about one of the issues or about a made-up issue, using the cuttings as a model.

♦ Ask the children to brainstorm some changes they would like to see implemented in the school. Make a list of them. Carry out a survey in other classes to find out which of these changes other children would also like to see carried out. The children could write to the headteacher with the results of the survey and a meeting could be arranged to discuss the possibility of implementation.

♦ Ask the children to come up with their own plan for improving an aspect of the local area. They could draw a map showing the location, a labelled plan of the change to take place and an advertising poster telling local people about the proposal. Each child/pair could present their idea to the rest of the class and the others could put forward their ideas for and against the plan.

The new supermarket

A large crowd has begun to gather outside Wilton's village hall. They are there to attend the public meeting between the residents of Wilton and a developer who wants to build a large supermarket on the edge of the village. Mrs Jackson and Mrs Parsonage are standing apart near the side entrance.

MRS JACKSON: *(whispering)* Who'd have thought that even old Ned Taylor would give up his precious time to come here tonight!

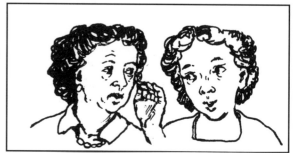

MRS PARSONAGE: *(sneering)* Humph, and I know why! His brother-in-law is a partner in the construction firm!

MRS JACKSON: *(still whispering)* Typical, that is! I bet he'll get a nice surprise in his bank account if he helps it all go ahead. Oh, no. Look out; here comes Norah!

NORAH: *(smiling and sounding happy)* Oh, hello you two. Why on earth are you hiding over here? You're missing all the excitement! Peter and Bob are getting very heated and they haven't even opened the doors yet *(laughing)*. Peter thinks we should all vote for the supermarket because he's heard that the company will build us a brand new village hall if we agree to it. But Bob is furious. He says once we let the supermarket in then all sorts of other companies will want to build here and our lovely quiet village will disappear for ever.

The sounds of angry, raised voices can be heard from the front of the hall.

MRS JACKSON: *(grabbing Mrs Parsonage by the arm)* Come on, we're missing all the action!

The three ladies race to the hall entrance door. There they see a very red-faced Peter shouting at an even redder-faced Bob.

PETER: *(shouting)* You seem to be missing the point! The supermarket will be right out on the edge of the village, closer to Bigtown than us. We've wanted a new village hall for years now – it might be our only chance to get it.

BOB: *(angry)* It's not me who's missing the point! It's you! Can't you see that this will just be the tip of the iceberg? The developers won't just stop with the supermarket – there'll be a DIY store, then a garden centre – you just wait and see – we'll have no peace!

✦ The new supermarket ✦

✦ Continue the play script about the new supermarket by completing the script below.

Bob and Peter's argument is soon interrupted by the arrival of the councillor, Mr Page, and Mrs Saville from the supermarket company.

MR PAGE: (*cheery smile*) Hello! Sorry we're late. I hope we haven't kept you waiting too long. Shall we go inside?

MRS PARSONAGE: (*whispering to Mrs Jackson*) Well, he certainly looks pleased with himself. Do you think he's made a deal with the supermarket?

MRS JACKSON: _____

_____

Everyone walks into the hall and takes a seat. Mr Page and Mrs Saville walk to the front of the hall and sit down at a large table. There is a lot of chatter as people settle themselves down. Suddenly Mr Page bangs his hand on the table.

MR PAGE: (*clears his throat loudly*) Can I have everyone's attention please? Thank you. Mrs Saville will now talk through the supermarket proposal in detail. We will then have time for questions.

MRS SAVILLE: (_____) Thank you Mr Page. Now I know that a lot of you are very worried about this proposal but I hope you will allow me time to explain it in more detail…

As Mrs Saville is explaining the supermarket plans, Mrs Jackson and Mrs Parsonage are having their own discussion at the back of the hall.

MRS PARSONAGE: (*whispering*) What do you think of the idea? Do you want the supermarket to be built?

MRS JACKSON: (*whispering*) _____

_____

MRS PARSONAGE: (_____) That's just what I think! What does Mike say about it?

MRS JACKSON: (*whispering*) _____

_____

MRS PARSONAGE: _____

_____

✦ Continue the play script in your own words on the back of this sheet.

◆ The new supermarket ◆

◆ Continue the play script about the new supermarket by completing the script below.

Bob and Peter's argument is soon interrupted by the arrival of the councillor, Mr Page, and Mrs Saville from the supermarket company.

MR PAGE: (*cheery smile*) Hello! Sorry we're late. I hope we haven't kept you waiting too long. Shall we go inside?

MRS PARSONAGE: (*whispering to Mrs Jackson*) Well, he certainly looks pleased with himself. Do you think he's made a deal with the supermarket?

MRS JACKSON: _____
                  _____

Everyone walks into the hall and takes a seat. Mr Page and Mrs Saville walk to the front of the hall and sit down at a large table. There is a lot of chatter as people settle themselves down. Suddenly Mr Page bangs his hand on the table.

MR PAGE: (_____) _____
                  _____
                  _____

MRS SAVILLE: (_____) _____
                  _____
                  _____

As Mrs Saville is explaining the supermarket plans, Mrs Jackson and Mrs Parsonage are having their own discussion at the back of the hall.

MRS PARSONAGE: (*whispering*) What do you think of the idea? Do you want the supermarket to be built?

MRS JACKSON: (*whispering*) _____
                  _____

MRS PARSONAGE: (*whispering*) _____
                  _____

MRS JACKSON: (*whispering*) _____
                  _____

MRS PARSONAGE: (_____) _____
                  _____

◆ Continue the play script in your own words on the back of this sheet.

Name _____

◆ The new supermarket ◆

◆ Continue the play script about the new supermarket by writing the script below. Include Mrs Jackson and Mrs Parsonage in the script. Make sure the reader is made aware of their views about the supermarket. Don't forget to include directions for the characters so the readers know how to read the parts.

Bob and Peter's argument is soon interrupted by the arrival of the councillor, Mr Page, and Mrs Saville from the supermarket company.

_____

_____

_____

Everyone walks into the hall and takes a seat. Mr Page and Mrs Saville walk to the front of the hall and sit down at a large table. There is a lot of chatter as people settle themselves down. Suddenly Mr Page bangs his hand on the table.

_____

_____

_____

As Mrs Saville is explaining the supermarket plans, Mrs Jackson and Mrs Parsonage are having their own discussion at the back of the hall.

_____

_____

_____

_____

◆ Continue the play script on the back of this sheet.

Photocopiable

Chapter 2

In the news – 2

 Literacy objectives

- To develop a journalistic style through considering:
  - balanced and ethical reporting
  - what is of public interest in events
  - the interests of the reader
  - selection and presentation of information.
  (Y6: T1, T15)
- To write a newspaper report. (Y6: T1, T16)

 Geography objectives

(Unit 16)
- To show an understanding of geographical processes relating to news items by writing a news report using interpretation of secondary sources.
- To use secondary sources.

 Resources

- Pictures of earthquake damage.
- Maps showing location and cities of Japan.
- Newspaper reports on natural disasters.

 Starting point: Whole class

- Tell the children that they are going to find out about an earthquake that took place in the city of Kobe in Japan. Use a world map to show the location of Japan in relation to the UK. Then use a map of Japan to locate Kobe.
- Ask the children to tell you what they know about earthquakes. Briefly discuss what causes them and the damage they can do. Show some pictures of earthquake damage.
- Explain that Japan is a country that experiences a lot of earthquakes. The people there spend a lot of money trying to predict earthquakes. Schools have regular earthquake escape drills and roads and buildings are built with earthquakes in mind.
- Explain that the Kobe earthquake, called the Great Hanshin Earthquake, occurred on 16th January 1995. It lasted only one minute but over 5,500 people died. Earlier, in 1923, the Great Kanto Earthquake in Tokyo killed over 143,000 people.

- To try and imagine what it must be like to be in an earthquake, the children are going to read several different pieces of information about the one at Kobe.

 Using the photocopiable text

- Enlarge the texts on page 12 or make enough copies for each pair to have a copy.
- Share the texts. What type of texts are they? (1 – diary extract, 2 – information book extract, 3 – transcript of a television news bulletin.)
- Discuss the content of each text. What information can we learn about the earthquake from each one? List the facts on the board, for example the date and time of the earthquake and the damage caused.
- Tell the children they are going to write a newspaper report about the earthquake using the information from the three texts. Remind them about journalistic style by sharing some newspaper clippings about other natural disasters. What headlines are used? How do the reports begin? In what tense are they written? What information do they give?
- Ask the children to think up some suitable headlines for the Kobe earthquake report. Write their ideas on the board. Discuss what they think might be of public interest in the event – what types of things would people want to know? Talk about how important it is that the report is unbiased and balanced – would the reader just want to know about one person's experiences, for example, or have a wider picture? How might the interest of the reader be sustained? Through the use of effective subheadings? Through eye-witness reports? By using pictures? Agree which information from the three texts would probably not be necessary in the report (for example, the fact that the earth is made up of several plates).
- Together, model how to write the beginning of the report. Then explain that they are now going to write the report themselves.

In the news – 2

 Group activities

Using the differentiated activity sheets

Activity sheet 1: This sheet is aimed at children who need a lot of support in writing a newspaper report. They are provided with a writing frame and a selection of words from which to choose to complete the report.

Activity sheet 2: This sheet is aimed at children who are more confident in writing a report. They are given suggestions for each paragraph.

Activity sheet 3: This sheet is aimed at more able children. They are required to write their own newspaper report using the information on page 12 without any support.

 Plenary session

✦ Share the responses to the activity sheets. Are the children agreed that they have included the most important and relevant facts in their reports? How has the interest of the reader been maintained? How effective are the headlines and/or pictures? What difficulties did they have when writing the reports? How were these overcome?

 Follow-up ideas for literacy

✦ Using the information on page 12, ask the children to imagine they were in Kobe on the day of the earthquake. Ask them to write a letter to a friend describing what happened.

✦ Ask the children to use information books, CD-Roms and the Internet to find more information about earthquakes. Their information could be made into an information book with contents and index pages for the class or school library.

✦ Ask the children to pretend they are reporters covering the news of the Kobe disaster. Role-play interviews with eye-witnesses. What types of questions will they ask these people? How can they record their answers? (Note form? Tape recorded?)

✦ Experiment with writing poems using personification, for example:
– a raging bull
– a howling wolf
– a thundering giant
– a violent earthquake.

 Follow-up ideas for geography

✦ Ask the children to collect newspaper reports about natural disasters around the world. Make a display of them, locating the places on a world map. Ask the children to find more information about these places. Why have the disasters occurred there? How have they affected the land and the people? How could they be prevented?

✦ Find out about local natural disasters such as recent flooding. Interview local people/ parents to find out how the flooding affected them.

✦ On a world map, mark the location of the main earthquake and volcano areas. Ask the children to find out about the 'Ring of Fire'. Use information books to find out about volcanoes and how they are formed. Share reports about recent volcanic eruptions – discuss how these have affected the physical and human features and resources of the area.

◆ The Kobe earthquake ◆

1

January 16th 1995

I am so thankful to be alive! A terrible earthquake occurred today. I awoke very suddenly at a quarter to 6 in the morning. The whole room was shaking. It was terrifying because I wasn't sure at first if I was just dreaming but then things began to fall off the shelves in my room and everything was crashing to the floor. I tried to stand up but it was impossible so I crawled along the floor that was rolling like a ship at sea. Some of the walls and floors were cracking open and I could hear the deafening crash of breaking glass outside. I eventually made it to the ground floor where everyone huddled together. We were too frightened to go outside. Later on someone told me the quake only lasted for a minute, but to me it seemed like hours!

2

What caused the earthquake?

The earth is made up of several large pieces (called plates) that fit together like a jigsaw puzzle. These plates are constantly moving very slowly against each other. The places where two plates meet are where nearly all earthquakes occur and most volcanoes are found.

The four main islands of Japan sit where four plates meet. It was a sudden movement along one of these boundaries that caused the earthquake in Kobe on January 16th, 1995.

Kobe Japan

3

"At 5.46 this morning a major earthquake struck Kobe. Many thousands of people are feared dead. Thousands of buildings and many main roads have been destroyed. The main rail link has also been badly damaged. Many fires have broken out which the fire brigades are struggling to contain due to massive damage to water pipes in the city. Water, gas and electricity supplies to nearly one million households have been cut off.

Many of the city's older multi-storey buildings are leaning at dangerous angles but more modern buildings seem to have survived. Already survivors who lost their homes have set up camps in several of the city's carparks. Eye-witnesses claim that there have been over 600 aftershocks following the quake. There will be more news on this terrible tragedy in our 10 o'clock bulletin tonight."

Activity 1   **Name** _____

✦ Newspaper report ✦

✦ Complete this newspaper report about the earthquake in Kobe using the words
   in the box at the bottom of the page. Draw a picture to go with the report.

Huge quake in _____!

Thousands are feared dead.

At 5.46 this morning a _____ earthquake hit the city of Kobe. It was so _____ that thousands of buildings have been_____

The main road and rail _____ to the city have been badly _____ and it is expected to take many _____ before transport returns to normal.

All water, electricity and _____ supplies have been cut off. It will be _____ weeks before these are restored. A spokesperson for the fire brigade said that they were

_____ to put out all the fires because of the lack of water supply to the

_____

Although the earthquake only lasted one _____ over 600 aftershocks were

_____

minute	destroyed	damaged	gas
terrible	struggling	months	many
violent	reported	links	city

Newspaper report

✦ Complete this newspaper report about the earthquake in Kobe.
The first paragraph has been done for you. Write about the following things:
 • paragraph 2: how the roads and railways have been affected
 • paragraph 3: the damage to gas, water and electricity supplies
 • paragraph 4: the fires
 • paragraph 5: what some of the survivors have done.

Huge quake rocks Kobe!

Thousands are feared dead. At 5.46 this morning a terrible earthquake hit the city of Kobe. The earthquake was so violent that thousands of buildings have been destroyed.

_____

_____

_____

_____

_____

_____

_____

_____

_____

_____

_____

_____

_____

_____

Photocopiable

Activity 3

 Newspaper report

✦ Using the information from the three sample texts, write a newspaper report about the earthquake at Kobe. Remember the following things:
  • use an attention-seeking headline
  • keep to the relevant facts
  • use paragraphs

Water – 1

 Literacy objectives

◆ To convey feelings, reflections or moods in a poem through the careful use of words and phrases. (Y5: T1, T16)

 Geography objectives

(Unit 11)
◆ To understand that water is a universal necessity.
◆ To list the uses for water.
◆ To understand the issue of wasting water.

 Resources

◆ Dictionaries and thesauruses.

 Starting point: Whole class

◆ Tell the children that they are going to read a poem about how we use water in our everyday lives. Explain that before sharing the poem, you want them to think of between five and ten things we use water for. Ask them to write a list of these and to do this as an individual task. Explain that as they read the poem you want them to see how many of the things they thought of are included in it.

 Using the photocopiable text

◆ Share an enlarged version of page 18 or provide each pair with a copy.
◆ Read the poem to the class as they follow it. What do they think of it? What is their favourite line? Why? How many different uses for water does the poem suggest? Make a class list and as the list is being made ask the children to tick off any of the same uses they have on their own list. Do they have any uses on their list that are not mentioned in the poem? Can they think of any other uses?
◆ Discuss the importance of and universal need for water. Ask questions such as 'Does everyone in the world need water?', 'Do plants and animals need water?', 'Do some countries have more water than others?', 'Why might this be?', 'Do some countries use water in different ways from us?' and 'Can we live without water?'

◆ Refer to the last four lines of the poem. What is the poet trying to tell us? Why might the water 'never return'? Talk about the problems of water pollution and how we need to store, clean and conserve water to maintain the levels we require. Discuss what happens after we have used water. Where does it go? What happens to it? How can we prevent wastage? How is it cleaned for reuse?
◆ Tell the children that you want them to write their own poems about how important water is to us and how we use it. Explain that they will be using verbs and adjectives in their poems. Ask the children to think of some adjectives that could be used to describe water. Write these on the board. Underline the words 'roaring' and 'shimmering' in the poems. How descriptive are these words? Does describing waves breaking with a 'roaring crash', for example, help us to build up an evocative image of the waves? Look at the list of adjectives the children thought of. Can some of these be more descriptive? Show them how they can use a thesaurus to find more descriptive words, for example, instead of 'refreshing' you might use 'invigorating', 'stimulating' or 'revivifying'.
◆ Ask the children to find verbs in the poem that tell us how we use water. Underline them. Can they suggest other verbs? Again, use a thesaurus to find alternatives.
◆ Finally, model how to create a poem using the lists of words. Explain that we want to make people aware of how important water is by using the most descriptive words and phrases that we can. For example:

> Water is invigorating, water is precious
> We use it to refresh and cleanse
> Water is powerful, water is sparkling
> We use it to sustain and flourish
> Without it we cannot survive.

 Group activities

Using the differentiated activity sheets

Activity sheet 1: This sheet is aimed at children who need a lot of support in writing their own poems. They are provided with a list of adjectives and verbs from which to choose.

Water – 1

Activity sheet 2: This sheet is aimed at children who are more confident with writing their own poems. They are required to use a thesaurus to find descriptive verbs and adjectives.

Activity sheet 3: This sheet is for more able children. They are required to write a two-verse poem using their own verbs and adjectives.

Plenary session

Share the responses to the activity sheets. How many different verbs and adjectives were used to describe water?

Are some words more descriptive than others? Why? What types of moods/feelings are created by the poems? Do they encourage people to conserve water/realise the value of water, for example?

Follow-up ideas for literacy

♦ Ask the children to find out from information books, the Internet and so on, how to conserve water. They could then write a set of instructions for the classroom or the home telling people how they can save water each day. The instructions could be presented as a poster.

♦ Share other poems about looking after the Earth's resources. An interesting collection is to be found in *Earthways, Earthwise – Poems on Conservation,* selected by Judith Nicholls, Oxford University Press.

♦ Tell the children how electricity is made using water. Ask them to make notes during your presentation. Then ask the children to use their notes to make a

flow diagram showing the stages in electricity production.

♦ Explore adjectives and verbs further. How many verbs, for example, can the children suggest to describe the actions of water? An excellent poem for this purpose is 'The Cataract of Lodore' by Robert Southey, part of which is presented in *The New Oxford Treasury of Children's Poems*, Oxford University Press.

♦ Challenge the children to write a description of water to explain to an alien what it is and how we use it!

Follow-up ideas for geography

♦ What evidence of water is there in the local area? Go on a walk around the neighbourhood, marking on a map any water sources and things associated with water – for example, ponds, rivers, streams, lakes, water fountains, swimming pools, fire hydrants, sewerage manholes, drinking fountains. Discuss the uses of each one and where the water comes from/goes to.

♦ Visit a farm to find out how crops/livestock are watered. How is water stored/transported? How much water is required each year?

♦ Use secondary sources to find out about the work of aid agencies in less economically developed

countries. Discuss how access to water varies in different parts of the world. Find out how improving the water supply can dramatically raise the living standards of the local people.

♦ Ask the children to think about what happens to the water that falls as rain. Where does it go – when it falls on our houses; when it falls on the land/rivers? How do people manage this water? Find out about the role of the water authorities and how homes are supplied with water.

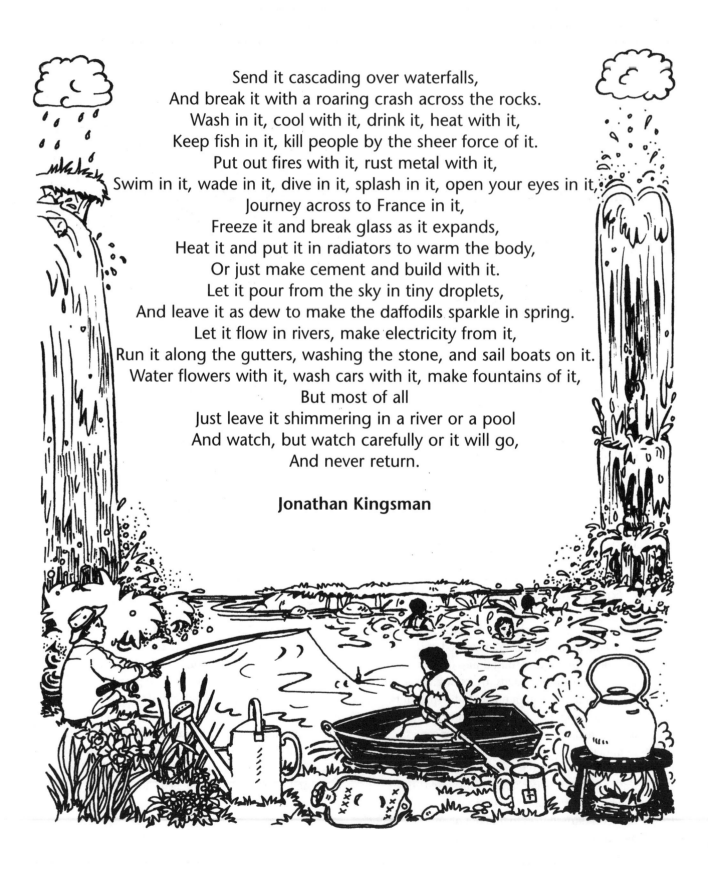

Send it cascading over waterfalls,
And break it with a roaring crash across the rocks.
Wash in it, cool with it, drink it, heat with it,
Keep fish in it, kill people by the sheer force of it.
Put out fires with it, rust metal with it,
Swim in it, wade in it, dive in it, splash in it, open your eyes in it,
Journey across to France in it,
Freeze it and break glass as it expands,
Heat it and put it in radiators to warm the body,
Or just make cement and build with it.
Let it pour from the sky in tiny droplets,
And leave it as dew to make the daffodils sparkle in spring.
Let it flow in rivers, make electricity from it,
Run it along the gutters, washing the stone, and sail boats on it.
Water flowers with it, wash cars with it, make fountains of it,
But most of all
Just leave it shimmering in a river or a pool
And watch, but watch carefully or it will go,
And never return.

Jonathan Kingsman

✦ W a t e r   p o e m ✦

✦ Complete the poem below using your own words or choosing words from the boxes.
  Use a dictionary and a thesaurus to help you.

Water is _____ , water is _____ (2 adjectives)

We use it to _____ and _____ (2 verbs)

Water is _____ , water is _____ (2 adjectives)

We use it to _____ and _____ (2 verbs)

Without water we wouldn't survive.

Adjectives		
cool	soft	new
refreshing	powerful	important
useful	fast	fresh
valuable	bubbly	chilly
wonderful	precious	dazzling
nice	free	deep

Verbs		
wash	cook	pour
splash	drink	rinse
clean	cool	float
swim	gargle	soothe
travel	live	bathe
play	build	grow

✦ Look at the last line of the poem again. Think of some sentences that
  might be more descriptive or show a stronger feeling. Write them
  below. One has been done for you.

Never waste it; always conserve it! _____

_____

_____

_____

✦ Water poem ✦

✦ Use a thesaurus to find more expressive words than those below
   that can be used to describe water. Write them in the boxes.

refreshing	valuable	bubbly	strong	good

wash	grow	splash	live	make

✦ Now select the best words to complete the poem below.

Water is _____, water is _____ (2 adjectives)

We use it to _____ and _____ (2 verbs)

Water is _____, water is _____ (2 adjectives)

We use it to _____ and _____ (2 verbs)

_____ (sentence)

✦ Water poem ✦

✦ Use a dictionary and a thesaurus to find the most descriptive words you can to complete the two verses of the poem below. Make sure you try to get across how important and precious water is to us and how we shouldn't waste it.

Water is _____, water is _____ (2 adjectives)

We use it to _____ and _____ (2 verbs)

Water is _____, water is _____ (2 adjectives)

We use it to _____ and _____ (2 verbs)

_____ (sentence)

Water is _____, water is _____ (2 adjectives)

We use it to _____ and _____ (2 verbs)

Water is _____, water is _____ (2 adjectives)

We use it to _____ and _____ (2 verbs)

_____ (sentence)

©Hopscotch Educational Publishing

Water – 2

 Literacy objectives

✦ To write instructional texts and try them out. (Y5: T1, T25)

 Geography objectives

(Unit 11)
✦ To know what is meant by 'usable water'.
✦ To understand the comparative importance of clean water and plentiful supply.
✦ To collect and analyse evidence.

 Resources

✦ Examples of instructional texts, such as recipes and games rules, as well as some science experiments instructions.
✦ Jars, water, measuring jug, soil/sand, teaspoon, plastic funnel, a drinking glass and a variety of different materials to use as filters, such as coffee filter papers, nylon tights, hessian, cotton, tissue paper, writing paper and so on.

 Starting point: Whole class

✦ Show the children a jar of water that has soil in it. Shake it and then pour it into a drinking glass. Pass the glass to someone and ask 'Would it be safe to drink this?' Discuss why not. Talk about how important it is to make sure the water we drink will not make us ill. Tell the children that in the early 19th century water supplies were not clean and people contracted diseases such as typhoid and cholera from drinking contaminated water.
✦ Discuss the term 'clean water' – it is not always the colour of water that tells us it may not be safe to drink it; there are microscopic things in the water, such as bacteria, that can cause illness.
✦ Discuss how in the past, villagers got their water from wells, ponds and streams. How might this water become contaminated? Discuss possible pollutants, such as someone throwing rubbish into the well, droppings from animals drinking at the water site and so on. Then discuss how our water supply might become polluted today, from factory leakages, sewage and so on. Explain that such pollution makes the water unusable.
✦ Tell the children how our drinking water is purified today through sedimentation, filtration, oxidation and disinfection to make it suitable for human consumption.

Discuss who carries out this service and how important it is to maintain a safe water supply.
✦ Tell the children that they are now going to find out a little more about how water can be cleaned by reading about a science experiment on filtering.

 Using the photocopiable text

✦ Share an enlarged version of page 24 or provide each pair with a copy.
✦ Share the text. Discuss each step of the experiment. Have the children carried out filtering experiments before? Discuss what happened.
✦ Explain that you would like to rewrite the information contained in the child's report as a set of instructions so that other people could also carry out the experiment.
✦ Revise the format and layout of instructions. Show the children the examples of instructions. Discuss the use of headings, subheadings, bullet points or numbering, labelled diagrams and the use of the imperative.
✦ Model how to write the instructions by working them out together. Use subheadings such as 'What you need' and 'What to do' and number each step. Reread the instructions. Are they clear enough for someone else to follow? Has anything important been left out? Ideally, try out the instructions and do the experiment yourselves.
✦ Tell the children that they are now going to write some more instructions for a different filtering experiment. Explain that after they have written their instructions, you want them to carry out the experiment to see if they work!

Group activities

Using the differentiated activity sheets

Activity sheet 1: This sheet is aimed at children who need a lot of support in writing a set of instructions. They are required to complete a writing frame using words from the given text.

Activity sheet 2: This sheet is aimed at children who need less support. They are required to complete more of the writing frame themselves.

Water – 2

Activity sheet 3: This sheet is for more able children who are confident enough to read the text and write their own set of instructions.

◆ Plenary session

◆ Share the responses to the activity sheets. Did the children carry out their instructions successfully? Can they see a need to change any of their instructions? Discuss the results of the experiment. Are some filters better than others? Discuss how important it is for water suppliers to make sure the filtering process they use ensures that the water is totally safe to use afterwards.

◆ Follow-up ideas for literacy

◆ Ask the children to write other sets of instructions, perhaps for class or school use, such as how to put PE apparatus away correctly or how to use a specific computer program.
◆ Challenge the children to write for a different audience by asking them to rewrite their instructions so that they are suitable for a younger child. Discuss the importance of diagrams and how these can help a non-reader or less able reader understand what to do.
◆ Ask the children to draw up a list of imperative verbs that might be suitable for science experiments, such

as 'put', 'stir', 'make', 'fill', 'cut' and 'measure'. Begin with examples in their own set of instructions and challenge them to find more. Collate the lists into a class display for the children to refer to when they are writing other instructions.
◆ Ask the children to make up a new game. It could be a PE game, a playground game or a board game. Ask them to write the instructions for it and give them to someone else to play. How clear and precise are they?

◆ Follow-up ideas for geography

◆ Ask the children to find out about water supplies in other countries. Do some places have more reliable and cleaner sources than others? What is being done to ensure everyone has clean water?
◆ Visit a sewage or water treatment plant. Ask the children to draw a flow diagram showing the main stages of the process.
◆ Locate places of very high and places of very low rainfall in the world. Discuss how some places need to conserve water more than others.
◆ Investigate water usage in the school. Is there too much waste? Discuss ways to reduce water usage – such as not cleaning things under a running tap,

repairing dripping taps, installing water efficient toilets, collecting rain water for watering plants and so on.

Our filtering experiment

We had to work out how to separate things from water.

We used two bowls, water, a colander, a tea-strainer, a funnel, a large jar, coffee filters, tea leaves, sand and peas.

First of all we filled one bowl with water and then we put the peas into the water. We had to decide how to separate the peas from the water. We used the colander. We tipped the bowl up and emptied it through the colander into the other bowl. The peas stayed in the colander and only the water went into the bowl.

Next, we stirred some tea leaves into a bowl of water. We poured the mixture through a tea-strainer to separate the tea leaves from the water.

Lastly, we mixed some sand into the water. We rested a funnel in the neck of a jar and we lined the funnel with a coffee filter paper. We poured the sand and water into the funnel. The sand got stuck on the filter paper and the water went through into the jar.

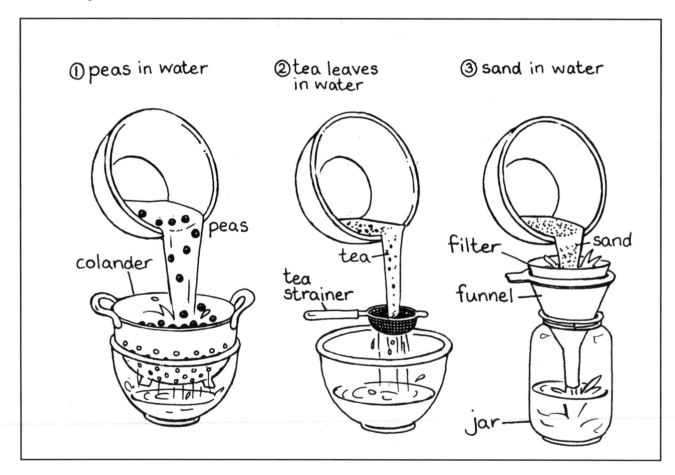

① peas in water ② tea leaves in water ③ sand in water

peas — colander

tea — tea strainer

filter — sand — funnel — jar

✦ Filtering ✦

✦ Read through the filtering experiment below. Use words from it to complete
  the set of instructions. Then try out the instructions yourself!

*We had to find out which material made
the best filter. We used a funnel, water,
soil, a teaspoon, a measuring jug and
some jars. We tested out the following
materials: coffee filter paper, nylon tights,
tissue paper, hessian and cotton fabric.*

*First we mixed a teaspoon of soil into
a jar containing 50ml of water. We put*

*the funnel into the neck of another jar and
then we lined the funnel with a coffee
filter paper. We poured the mixture into
the funnel and waited until all the water
had dripped through into the jar. We
wrote down what happened.*

*We repeated the experiment using
each of the other filter materials in turn.*

Instructions for filtering experiment

You will need:

a f_____, water, j____, a t_____, a measuring _____, some
soil, coffee _____ paper, tissue _____, nylon _____,
h_____ and some cotton _____

What to do:

1. Measure out 50ml of _____ using the measuring jug.

2. Put the water into a _____

3. Measure a teaspoonful of _____

4. Stir the soil into the _____

5. Put the _____ into the neck of another jar.

6. Line the funnel with a _____ filter paper.

7. _____ the mixture into the funnel.

8. Record what _____

9. Repeat steps 1 to 8 using different materials in the funnel.

©Hopscotch Educational Publishing

◆ Filtering ◆

◆ Read through the filtering experiment below. Use the text to complete the set of instructions. Then try out the instructions yourself!

We had to find out which material made the best filter. We used a funnel, water, soil, a teaspoon, a measuring jug and some jars.

We tested out the following materials: coffee filter paper, nylon tights, tissue paper, hessian and cotton fabric.

First we mixed a teaspoon of soil into a jar containing 50ml of water. We put the funnel into

the neck of another jar and then we lined the funnel with a coffee filter paper.

We poured the mixture into the funnel and waited until all the water had dripped through into the jar. We wrote down what happened.

We repeated the experiment using each of the other filter materials in turn.

Instructions for filtering experiment

You will need:

What to do:

1. Measure out 50ml of _____ using the measuring jug.

2. Put the water into a _____

3. Measure a teaspoonful of _____

4. Stir the soil into the _____

5.

6.

7.

8. Record what _____

9. Repeat steps 1 to 8 using different materials in the funnel.

◆ Filtering ◆

◆ Read through the filtering experiment below. Use the text to write a set of instructions to repeat the experiment. Then try out the instructions yourself!

We had to find out which material made the best filter.

We used a funnel, water, soil, a teaspoon, a measuring jug and some jars. We tested out the following materials: coffee filter paper, nylon tights, tissue paper, hessian and cotton fabric.

First we mixed a teaspoon of soil into a jar containing 50ml of water. We put the funnel into the neck of another jar and then we lined the funnel with a coffee filter paper.

We poured the mixture into the funnel and waited until all the water had dripped through into the jar. We wrote down what happened.

We repeated the experiment using each of the other filter materials in turn.

Instructions for filtering experiment

_____

_____

_____

_____

_____

_____

_____

_____

_____

_____

Chapter 5

The environment

Literacy objectives

+ To understand the differences between literal and figurative language. (Y5: T2, T10)
+ To use the structures of poems read to write extensions of these by substituting own words and ideas. (Y5: T2, T12)

Geography objectives

(Unit 13)
+ To develop an awareness of the quality of the environment and further develop a sense of place.

Resources

+ Some pictures of chemical works, cooling towers and power stations at night.

Starting point: Whole class

+ Ask the children to look out from the classroom windows (or another suitable place in the school). Ask them to tell you what buildings and other objects are visible. List them on the board. How would they describe these things and the scene in general? Ask them to tell you suitable words and phrases. Write these on the board. Finally, ask the children to tell you how it makes them feel when they are looking at the scene. Write these ideas on the board as well.
+ Sit the class down again. Ask them to close their eyes and think of another scene (perhaps from a recent holiday or from their home) that makes them feel happy. Why does looking at this scene make them feel this way? What is so good about it? How different is this scene from the one they saw from the school window?
+ Tell them that they are now going to share a poem about another person who is looking out of his or her window at home.

Using the photocopiable text

+ Enlarge the text on page 30 or arrange for each pair of children to have a copy.
+ Read the poem to them as they follow it. Discuss the content. Why do the poets say it's beautiful three times and then decide it's ugly?

+ Show the class some pictures of factories at night. Discuss how colourful the lights can be against a dark sky. How do the poets describe the lights from the power station? The flames? The steam? Why do the children think these words have been used?
+ Underline 'like runny paint on a paper', 'like a dragon's breath' and 'like a white scarf'. Tell the children that these phrases are 'similes'. Explain the term. What other similes could be used instead? How else could these things be described? Ask the children to make some suggestions. Write them on the board.
+ Explain that this type of language is called 'figurative' and that authors use it to make their writing more descriptive and to help the reader understand better how something might look or feel. Ask them to tell you what the lights, works and towers might literally look like, for example 'The lights are red, yellow and blue. They shine on the water.'
+ Look at the lists written earlier about what the children can see from their window. Model how to write some sentences using similes for these things, for example 'The terraced houses look like soldiers all standing to attention.' Ask the children to suggest some more.
+ Can a place be both good and bad, ugly and beautiful – as in the poem? What things seen from the school window are ugly? What is beautiful? Do they enjoy the scene they are looking at? Why/why not?
+ Together, write a poem modelled on 'From My Window' using the children's ideas about what can be seen from the school window.
+ Tell the children they are now going to write a similar poem of their own.

Group activities

Using the differentiated activity sheets

Activity sheet 1: This sheet is aimed at children who need a lot of support in writing a poem. They are required to complete a line in each verse of a given poem, choosing phrases from a selection given or using their own words.

Activity sheet 2: This sheet is aimed at children who are more confident in writing a poem. They are required to complete several lines in each verse with no support.

The environment

Activity sheet 3: This sheet is for more able children. They are required to write three verses of a poem in the style of the first verse. No support is given.

 Plenary session

✦ Share the responses to the activity sheets. How many different similes did the children come up with? Which descriptions do they like best? Why? What did they find most difficult about writing the poem? Are they pleased with the results? How could they improve? What could they write about next?

 Follow-up ideas for literacy

✦ Ask the children to write poems about scenes they see from other windows such as at home, using the same structure and form as 'From My Window'.

✦ Explore metaphors. Make a collection of poems that use metaphors and similes. Poems include 'The Sea' by James Reeves (*The New Oxford Treasury of Children's Poems*, Oxford University Press), 'The Eagle' by Alfred, Lord Tennyson (*The Puffin book of Classic Verse*), 'Silver' by Walter de la Mare (*I like this Poem*, Puffin) and 'Charlotte's Dog' by Kit Wright (*Cat Among the Pigeons*, Viking Kestrel).

✦ Ask the children to write a descriptive passage about a view from a window or door. Present the writing by making 'lift-the-flaps' or 'fold-out windows and doors' with the writing inside. They could perhaps write about a scene they would like to see out of their own window, such as a beautiful tropical island!

✦ Discuss how the view from a window could be improved. Ask the children to design a poster telling people not to drop litter on beaches, for example.

 Follow-up ideas for geography

✦ Visit an area that contrasts with the children's own local area. Ask them to write words and phrases to describe it. How does it compare with their own area? Is this a place they would prefer to be? Why/why not? How could this place be improved?

✦ Ask the children to make a map of the area seen from their school window. They could use a key to colour the different land uses (such as green for parks, lawns etc, blue for houses, red for businesses) and symbols to represent features such as churches, bridges, post offices, bus stops and so on.

✦ Ask the children to carry out a questionnaire survey of the parents in their school to find out what they think about the quality of the local environment. Are they happy with the facilities? Is traffic a problem? Are any areas polluted? Try and follow up any issues raised with the local council.

✦ Make a display of views from windows. Use postcards/ magazine pictures. Pin them up around a local or regional map. Join the pictures to the locations on the map with string. Ask the children to find information about these places.

From My Window

Lights of the power station
at night
over the water
like runny paint on a paper.

It's beautiful.

Flames from the chemical works
at night
against the sky
like a dragon's breath.

It's beautiful.

Steam from the cooling towers
at night
covering the Moon
like a white scarf.

It's beautiful.

I live near the power station.
I live near the chemical works.
I live near the cooling towers.
At night
it hurts to breathe.

It's ugly.

Martyn Wiley and Ian McMillan

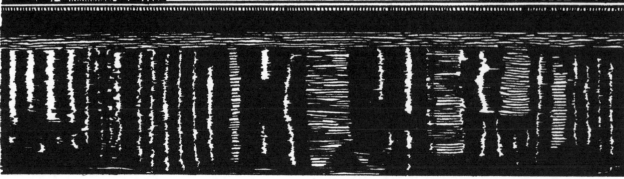

©Hopscotch Educational Publishing

◆ My poem ◆

◆ Complete the poem below. Use your own words or those from the box.
Use a dictionary to help you.

From the window...

Waves of the sea
at daybreak
sparkle and shimmer

like _____

It's lovely.

Pebbles of the seashore
at daybreak
are round and perfect

like_____

It's lovely.

Grass in the sand dunes
at daybreak
stands tall and bright

like_____

It's lovely.

Litter on the beach
at daybreak
scattered here and there

like_____

It's disgraceful!

dirt smudges on hands	jewels in a crown	plasters on a scabby knee
hundreds of diamonds	cobbles in a lane	green garden statues
freckles on a face	a miniature forest	stars in the sky

✦ My poem ✦

✦ Complete the poem below using your own words. Use a dictionary to help you.

From the window...

Waves of the sea
at day break
sparkle and shimmer
like stars in a dark sky.

It's lovely.

Pebbles of the seashore
at daybreak
are _____
like_____

It's _____

Grass in the sand dunes
at _____
_____
like_____

It's _____

Litter on the beach
at _____
_____
like_____

It's _____

©Hopscotch Educational Publishing

✦ My poem ✦

✦ Complete the poem below using your own ideas. Make sure you use similes in each verse. In the last verse write about something that is ugly in the scene. Use a dictionary to help you.

From the window...

Waves of the sea
at day break
sparkle and shimmer
like stars in a dark sky.

It's lovely.

_____
_____
_____
_____

It's _____

_____
_____
_____
_____

It's _____

_____
_____
_____
_____

It's _____

Traffic

 ## Literacy objectives

+ To compare writing which informs and persuades, considering:
  – the deliberate use of ambiguity, half-truth, bias
  – how opinion can be disguised to seem like fact.
  (Y5: T3, T13)
+ To write a commentary on an issue, setting out and justifying a point of view. (Y5: T3, T18)

 ## Geography objectives

(Unit 12)
+ To discuss an issue in an informed way using a range of evidence to arrive at an informed view about an issue.
+ To be aware of the range of views people hold about an issue.
+ To understand how places can be managed and improved.

 ## Resources

+ Some local or national newspaper reports about traffic issues.

 ## Starting point: Whole class

+ The children are going to look at some information about a village that has traffic problems. But before they do this, they should think about the traffic in their own locality. Do they think there is a problem in their area? Do they think too much traffic uses the main street? Do vehicles travel too fast? Do lots of vans and trucks go through their area? What problems can this cause? Do they feel safe crossing the roads? Is it important, for example, for shop owners and businesses to be able to have things delivered? Share the children's ideas and opinions. Talk about the fact that different people can hold very different views about the same issue.
+ If you have any newspaper clippings about traffic issues, spend some time discussing an issue and asking the children their opinions on it. Which people do they side with? Why?
+ Explain that you now want them to look at the problems faced by another place to compare it with their own area.

Using the photocopiable text

+ Share an enlarged version of page 36 or provide each pair with a copy.
+ Read through the texts together, discussing any difficult words. Which text is the letter to the editor of a newspaper? Which one is an information leaflet? Discuss the content of each text. What are they trying to tell us?
+ Look at the letter to the editor in more detail. Discuss the opinions expressed. Why do they think the author began the letter with 'This is just what we've all been waiting for!'? Is the deliberate ambiguity designed to grab our attention? Discuss the sentence beginning with 'It's no surprise...' Does this suggest that perhaps the people living in the town have had other unwanted plans foisted upon them by the council? What is the author trying to persuade his readers to do?
+ Compare this letter with the other texts. Is the newspaper article unbiased? Have the children been persuaded towards one view or the other? Why/ why not?
+ Ask the children to consider the 'fors' and 'againsts' as suggested in the texts. List them on the board. Can they think of any others?

For
Quicker deliveries to shops
New safe cycle path

Against
More traffic through the town
More chance of road accidents

+ Tell the children that it is only by considering the 'fors' and 'againsts' of an issue that we can make an informed decision about something. Do they feel they have enough information about the new road at Blareton to help them decide whether it is a good idea or not? What else might they want to find out about it?
+ Using the lists, model how to write a point of view either for or against the road scheme. Show them how to use connectives such as 'firstly', 'therefore', 'whereas' and 'surely' to express their point of view. Use numbering or bullet points to structure the writing.

Traffic

 Group activities

Using the differentiated activity sheets

Activity sheet 1: This sheet is aimed at children who need a lot of support in setting out and justifying a point of view. They are given lists of reasons for and against the issue and a writing frame in which to complete the commentary.

Activity sheet 2: This sheet is aimed at children who have more confidence in setting out a point of view. They are required to complete lists of reasons for and against the issue and then write their own commentary.

Activity sheet 3: This sheet is for more able children. They are required to write their own lists of reasons for and against as well as a commentary, without any support.

 Plenary session

Share the responses to the activity sheets. Were all the children able to find reasons for and against the issue? How persuasive do they consider their presentations of their points of view to be? How could they make them more so?

 Follow-up ideas for literacy

✦ Ask the children to design a poster persuading people either for or against the conversion of the High Street into a pedestrianised area. What techniques will they use to make it eye-catching? How much text will they put on the poster? Will they include pictures? How important is the size and colour of the text?

✦ Carry out a survey to find out about any concerns others have about the school, for example too much litter in the playground or safety issues about car parking. Ask the children to interview parents, children and teachers to find out their thoughts on the issue. Then ask them to write a newspaper style report on it. Publish the reports. Try to find ways to solve the issues.

✦ Ask the children to collect local and national newspaper stories about traffic problems. Make a class collection. Compare how the stories have been presented. Is bias evident? Do they consider they have all the relevant facts to make an informed decision about the issue?

 Follow-up ideas for geography

✦ Visit the local High Street. Ask the children to record the number and type of vehicles passing in, say, 20 minutes within certain time periods (for example starting at 9am, 11am and 2pm). They could present their data in a graph using graphing software. Discuss the results. Are some times of the day busier than other? Why might this be? What types of vehicles are most common? Do they consider the volume of traffic too heavy through the area? Why/why not?

✦ Devise a questionnaire to ask local people/parents regarding the feasibility of a traffic improvement scheme suitable for the local area, such as traffic calming measures outside the school, pedestrianising the High Street or putting in place improved measures to reduce speed, such as more signs and road markings. Discuss the results. Write to the local council about the results.

This is just what we've all been waiting for! Another new road is going to be built through our town, yippee!! It's no surprise to us all to learn that the road serves no purpose at all to those of us who live here – it's going to be built purely to join the industrial estate on the east of the town with the one on the west. Why they can't continue to use the ring road I'll never know! Now all the heavy goods vehicles will be able to cut across the town instead of having to go round it. What kind of madness is this? It's a fact that Blareton already has too much traffic thundering through it. Will it take a child to be killed before the council sits up and takes notice? I want you to join me in trying to put a stop to this stupid planning application. Send your letters of disagreement to Mr J Casey, Council Offices, High St, Blareton.

Mr Geoff Gillingham, Read St, Blareton.

SUPPORT OUR NEW ROAD

Plans for our long-awaited new road joining our two industrial estates have finally been drawn up.

At last businesses will not have to make a four-mile detour just to get from one estate to the other. This means that deliveries will be quicker and more efficient. There will be more opportunities for businesses to work together and this may create more employment for our town.

This means that companies like Perfect Paints will no longer have to make long journeys around the ring road just to make deliveries to shops at either end of the town.

The new road will also have a cycle path which means cyclists will be able to get right into the centre of town in safety. Pledge your support for the new road by coming to the planning meeting at the Council Offices, 7pm, Wednesday 7th June.

The Blareton Express

Planned new road fuels anger

Council offices besieged!
The planned new road through Blareton has created a storm of protests from angry residents, many of whom stood outside Blareton council offices all day today.

A spokesperson for the protestors said that many of the residents were strongly against the building of a new road through the town.

"We don't need another road. It serves no real purpose at all. All it will succeed in doing is encouraging even more traffic through our already busy town."

The protestors were carrying placards and were chanting "No more roads. Keep our town safe" for two hours before councillor James Casey appeared and agreed to talk to the crowd.

Mr Casey said that the road was a vital link between our two industrial estates – without it, he said, some of the businesses had threatened to leave.

The protestors were not convinced. They plan to picket the council offices every day until the road plans are abandoned.

✦ Traffic problems ✦

✦ Wigton Council wants to close its High Street to traffic and make the road into a pedestrianised area with seating and plants. Read these notes on the pros and cons of the idea.

FOR	**AGAINST**
• It will allow people to feel more relaxed when shopping. • It will reduce fumes from vehicles. • The area will look much better. • Restaurants could have seating outside. • It will be safer for pedestrians. • People might take more pride in the area. • It will encourage more people to shop in the town.	• It will make it much more difficult for deliveries to be made to the shops. • Drivers will become annoyed at having to make detours around High Street – this could cause more traffic problems in other areas. • If people are unable to park near the shops they might go elsewhere to shop. • It may encourage people to hang around the area and cause damage.

✦ Use these ideas and some of your own to write what you think should happen to the High Street and why.

I think that Wigton should/ should not (delete one) close the High Street to traffic because:

Firstly, I think that _____

_____

_____

Secondly, I believe that _____

_____

_____

Thirdly, I think that _____

_____

_____

And finally, and most importantly, I think _____

_____

_____

◆ Traffic problems ◆

◆ Wigton Council wants to close its High Street to traffic and make the road into a pedestrianised area with seating and plants. Add to these notes on the pros and cons of the idea.

FOR	AGAINST
• It will allow people to feel more relaxed when shopping.	• It will make it much more difficult for deliveries to be made to the shops.
• It will reduce fumes from vehicles.	• If people are unable to park near the shops they might go elsewhere to shop.
•	•
•	
•	•
•	
•	

◆ Use these ideas. Write what you think should happen to the High Street and why.

I think that Wigton should/should not (delete one) *close the High Street to traffic for the following reasons:*

_____

_____

_____

_____

_____

_____

_____

_____

_____

_____

_____

_____

Activity 3

✦ Traffic problems ✦

✦ Wigton Council wants to close its High Street to traffic and make the road
into a pedestrianised area with seating and plants. List some reasons for the
idea and some reasons against it.

FOR	AGAINST
•	•
•	•
•	•
•	•
•	

✦ Now use these ideas to write what you think should happen to the High Street and why.

_____

_____

_____

_____

_____

_____

_____

_____

_____

_____

_____

_____

_____

_____

_____

_____

Mountain environments – 1

 ## Literacy objectives

+ To revise work on contracting sentences (Y6: T2, S4)
+ To make notes in order to make a summary of information read.

 ## Geography objectives

(Unit 15)
+ To investigate how mountain environments are similar and different in nature across a range of places and scales.
+ To use secondary sources.

 ## Resources

+ World maps showing the location of the Himalayas, the Alps and Snowdonia.
+ Pictures of the three mountain areas.

 ## Starting point: Whole class

+ Tell the children they are going to find out about three different mountain areas of the world. Write the three areas on the board – the Himalayas, the Alps and Snowdonia. Ask the children to tell you what they already know about any of these places. Use maps to locate the regions and discuss how far away they are from where the children live. Show the pictures of the three regions.
+ Explain that you want them to make a summary of information about the three regions and to do this, they will be revising how to make notes.

 ## Using the photocopiable text

+ Enlarge the texts on page 42 or photocopy enough for each child to have a copy. Explain that the texts are extracts taken from an information book. Share the texts discussing any difficult words.
+ Ask the children to tell you how they might go about making a summary of information on the two regions. How might they make their notes – would they write in full sentences, for example?
+ Explain that you are going to show them how to make notes from each paragraph of the texts. Ask them to scan the texts quickly – what do they notice about the content of the paragraphs in both texts? (Paragraph 1 is

about location and general information; 2 – climate; 3 – vegetation; and 4 – people.) Write these on the board as separate headings and explain that you are now going to help them write some notes under each heading.
+ Reread the first paragraph on the Himalayas. What information do they think is the most important? Underline this. Then model how to write the notes, reminding them how to contract the sentences, leaving out the unimportant words. For example:

Himalayas
Location and general information
world's largest mountain area
southern Asia
2,400km long
Afghanistan, Pakistan, India, Tibet, Nepal, Bhutan
Mt Everest – world's highest mountain (8,848m)
K2 – world's second highest (8,611m)
Kangchenjunga – 3rd highest (8,585m)

+ Repeat the process for the other paragraphs, agreeing and underlining the most important information together. The children could work together in pairs to summarise the information on the Alps or this could also be done as a whole-class activity.
+ Discuss any similarities and differences they notice in the two mountain areas. For example, the valley areas are warmer in both places. The Himalayas are much higher than the Alps.
+ Tell the children that they are now going to write their own summary on the third mountain area, Snowdonia, in a similar way.

 ## Group activities

Using the differentiated activity sheets

Activity sheet 1: This sheet is aimed at children who need a lot of support in making notes. They are required to use underlined words to complete the writing frame.

Activity sheet 2: This sheet is for children who are more confident in making notes. They are still given support, however, in the provision of headings and underlined words.

Literacy through geography

Mountain environments - 1

Activity sheet 3: This sheet is for more able children. They are required to make their own notes without any support.

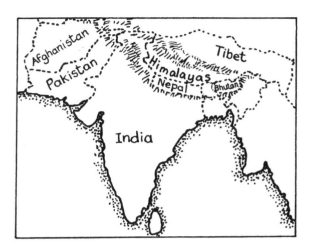

 Plenary session

Share the responses to the activity sheets. Are the children agreed on the most important things to include in their notes? Did they remember to use contracted sentences? Discuss the similarities and differences between Snowdonia and the other two mountain environments discussed at the beginning of the lesson.

◆ *Follow-up ideas for literacy*

- Ask the children to imagine they have visited one or all three of the mountain areas. Using pictures from books and so on, the children could write postcards and/or letters back home.
- Go for a walk up some steep hills! Ask the children to use this experience to help them write a story about being a mountain climber. Read true accounts.
- Make a class collection of mountain words. Use the list to create some poems.
- Share newspaper reports about mountain experiences such as mountaineering, mountain

rescues and volcanic eruptions. Ask the children to write their own newspaper report about a real or imaginary event.
- Share stories about the yeti or abominable snowman! Challenge the children to invent their own mountain creature. They could draw, label and describe it.
- Ask the children to use information books and the Internet to find out about the animals that inhabit mountainous regions. They could make class or individual books.

◆ *Follow-up ideas for geography*

- Ask the children to use information books, CD-Roms and the Internet to find more information about each of the three mountain areas. They could work in groups, concentrating on a different region each and then prepare a talk to give to the rest of the class.
- Find out about the other mountains in the world. Use maps to locate the highest mountains in each continent/country. Make a display showing their location in relation to the UK.
- Find out about specific weather related conditions in mountains, such as blizzards, avalanches and

snowdrifts. Discuss what impact they might have on the people who live there and those who are visiting.
- Contact tourist information/travel agencies for travel information to and in the three mountain regions. Make comparisons between the ease and modes of travel. The children could design a poster to entice people to visit an area.

The Himalayas

The world's largest mountain area, the Himalayas, lies in southern Asia. It stretches for over 2,400km from Afghanistan and Pakistan, through India, Tibet, Nepal and Bhutan. The Himalayas contain Mount Everest, the world's highest mountain (8,848m) and 12 other peaks over 8,000m, including K2 (8,611m) – the world's second highest mountain, Kangchenjunga (8,585m) – the world's third highest mountain and Nanga Parbat (8,126m).

The Himalayas have winter from October to February, summer from March to June and a very wet (monsoon) season from June to September. But the climate depends on altitude – it ranges from subtropical through temperate (2,130m) to alpine at 3,660m. There is a line of permanent snow at 5,030m. The southern slopes have very high rainfall whereas the northern slopes are very dry.

On the lower slopes there are thick forests of mixed deciduous and evergreen trees. Above these are deciduous trees. These give way to conifer and rhododendron forests from about 3,000 – 4,000m. Then come the alpine pastures and the permanent snow line.

There is a huge variety of people living in the region. Islam, Hinduism and Buddhism are the main religions. Most people live on the low slopes where the climate is mild and the soil is fertile. Grain and fruit are grown in fields and terraces.

The Alps

The Alps are Europe's most extensive mountain system. They are 800km long and form part of nine countries: France, Italy, Switzerland, Germany, Austria, Slovenia, Croatia, Bosnia and Hercegovina and Yugoslavia. The highest mountain in the Alps is Mont Blanc (4,807m) and the most famous mountain is the Matterhorn (4,477m) a steep-sided pyramid shape, making it a great challenge for climbers.

There are extreme differences in the climate within the Alps. The valleys are warmer and drier than the higher slopes. On the lower slopes the temperature in January is -5 °C – +8 °C and in July it is 15 °C – 24 °C. Rainfall is higher on the northern slopes.

Deciduous trees grow on the lower slopes. Higher up, coniferous trees grow. Between the tree line and the snow line, are alpine meadows.

Tourism is the main source of employment in the Alps. About 100 million people visit them every year for skiing and walking holidays. There are also farming, mining and manufacturing in the region.

◆ S n o w d o n i a ◆

◆ Use the underlined words to complete the notes on Snowdonia.

> ### Snowdonia
>
> Snowdonia is a _National Park_ in _Wales_. It covers an area of _2,171 square km_. The area is best known for its mountains and it includes Yr Wyddfa (_Snowdon_) (_1,085m_), the highest peak in England and Wales in the north, and Pen-y-Gader (892m) in the south.
>   Snowdonia has _mild winters_ and _cool summers_. _Rainfall_ comes _throughout_ the year. Annual mean temperatures range from _4˚C_ in _January_ to _16˚C_ in _July/August_.
>
> _Low-lying_ _areas_ consist of _moors_, _bogs_ and _meadows_. Further up are _deciduous_ and _coniferous woodlands_ and finally there are _arctic alpines_ such as the Snowdon Lily.
>
> _Tourism, mining_ (especially slate), _farming_ and _forestry_ are the _main industries_ in the region. The climb to the summit of Snowdon attracts 500,000 visitors a year.

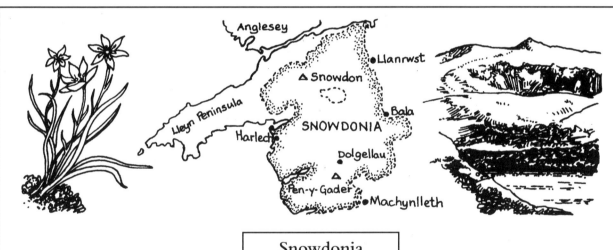

Snowdonia

Location and general information
National Park, Wales
area of _____ square km
highest peak England and Wales – _____
(_____ m)

Vegetation
low areas –
_____
deciduous and _____ woodlands
arctic alpines

Climate
mild _____, cool _____
rainfall throughout _____
4˚C – _____
16˚C – _____

People
main industries – tourism, _____,
_____ and _____

Snowdonia

✦ Use the underlined words to help you make notes about Snowdonia.

Snowdonia

Snowdonia is a <u>National Park</u> in <u>Wales</u> situated in the counties of Gwynedd and Conwy.

It covers an area of <u>2,171 square km</u>. The area is best known for its mountains and it includes Yr Wyddfa (<u>Snowdon</u>) <u>(1085m)</u>, the highest peak in England and Wales in the north, and Pen-y-Gader (892m) in the south.

Snowdonia has <u>mild winters</u> and <u>cool summers</u>. <u>Rainfall</u> comes <u>throughout</u> the <u>year</u> but varies through the region, for example, the summit of Snowdon may have 5,080mm a year but the coastline, 12 miles away, only has 760mm. Annual mean temperatures range from <u>4°C</u> in <u>January</u> to <u>16°C</u> in <u>July/August</u>.

<u>Low</u>-lying <u>areas</u> consist of <u>moors</u>, <u>bogs</u> and <u>meadows</u>. Further up are <u>deciduous</u> and <u>coniferous woodlands</u> and finally there are <u>arctic alpines</u> such as the Snowdon Lily. <u>Tourism</u>, <u>mining</u> (especially slate), <u>farming</u> and <u>forestry</u> are the <u>main industries</u> in the region. The population grows from 25,000 in winter to about 80,000 in summer. The climb to the summit of Snowdon attracts 500,000 visitors a year.

Snowdonia

Location and general information

_____
_____
_____
_____

Vegetation

_____
_____
_____
_____

Climate

_____
_____
_____
_____

People

_____
_____
_____
_____

Snowdonia

✦ Read through the information below. Underline the important words.
Use these words to make notes about Snowdonia.

Snowdonia

Snowdonia is a National Park in Wales situated in the counties of Gwynedd and Conwy. It covers an area of 2,171 square km. The area is best known for its mountains and it includes Yr Wyddfa (Snowdon) (1,085m), the highest peak in England and Wales in the north and Pen-y-Gader (892m) in the south.

Snowdonia has mild winters and cool summers. Rainfall comes throughout the year but varies through the region, for example, the summit of Snowdon may have 5,080mm a year but the coastline, twelve miles away, only has 760mm.

Annual mean temperatures range from 4°C in January to 16°C in July/August.

Low-lying areas consist of moors, bogs and meadows. Further up are deciduous and coniferous woodlands and finally there are arctic alpines such as the Snowdon Lily.

Tourism, mining (especially slate), farming and forestry are the main industries in the region. The population grows from 25,000 in winter to about 80,000 in summer. The climb to the summit of Snowdon attracts 500,000 visitors a year.

_____

_____

_____

_____

_____

_____

_____

_____

_____

_____

_____

_____

_____

Photocopiable

Mountain environments – 2

Literacy objectives

- To build a bank of useful terms and phrases for argument. (Y6: T2, W8)
- To recognise how arguments are constructed to be effective. (Y6: T2, T15)
- To identify the features of balanced written arguments. (Y6: T2, T16)
- To write a balanced argument. (Y6: T2, T19)

Geography objectives

(Unit 15)
- To understand that the effects of tourism can be significant in a given area and be both good and bad.

Resources

- Pictures of people using mountainous areas for skiing, walking, rock climbing and so on.

Starting point: Whole class

- Ask the children if they have ever been to a mountainous area on holiday – for skiing, walking or rock climbing, for example. Ask them where they went and what types of things they did there. Show the picture collection and discuss whether they have done, or seen other people doing, those things.
- Tell them that they are going to look at the effects of tourists visiting areas such as these. Ask them to suggest two good things about people visiting an area and two bad things. Write their ideas on the board. Tell them that they will now read some letters written to the editor of a newspaper that might give them some more ideas. Ask them to tell you why they think people might want to have letters published in a newspaper.

Using the photocopiable text

- Share an enlarged version of page 48 or provide each pair with a copy.
- Share the letters. What are the letters all about? What sort of place do they think Ben and Marian live in? Where might it be?

- Draw two columns on the board headed 'for tourism' and 'against tourism'. Go through each letter again and write the points mentioned in the appropriate column. Can anything else be added to the lists from the children's brainstorm at the beginning of the lesson?
- Explain that letters written to a newspaper editor are expressing a point of view. They often express an opinion for or against an issue. Consider Ben's letter – is he for or against tourism? And Marian's letter? Discuss how her letter tries to present both sides of the argument, making it more balanced. Ask the children to tell you whether they think it is important to hear both sides of an argument before they make up their own minds about an issue. Why?
- Tell them that they are going to write their own letter about the good and bad effects of tourism. Underline the following words in Ben's letter: 'similarly', 'equally' and 'furthermore'. Write these on the board. Explain that to write an argument well it is a good idea to use words that help construct the argument more effectively. Discuss how the underlined words can help someone express points of view that are in agreement with each other. Ask the children to think of other words that could be used, for example 'additionally', 'also', 'as well as', 'in addition to' and 'moreover'. Add these to the list and write the heading 'Words that agree with the argument'.
- Underline 'on the other hand' in Marian's letter. Explain how this expression helps to present the opposite point of view. Make a list of similar words, such as 'conversely', 'in contrast', 'however', 'nevertheless' and 'contrary to'.
- Underline 'clearly' and 'therefore'. List words that can be used to sum up an argument, such as 'finally', 'in conclusion', 'to sum up', 'in closing' and 'lastly'.
- Model how a letter to the editor might begin by agreeing the first paragraph together. For example, 'I am writing to express my opinion about the tourists in our area. Firstly I want to point out that...'

Group activities

Using the differentiated activity sheets

Activity sheet 1: This sheet is aimed at children who need a lot of support in writing a balanced argument. They are provided with sentences about the good and bad effects of tourism and they have to use these sentences within a given writing frame.

Mountain environments – 2

Activity sheet 2: This sheet is aimed at children who are more confident in writing an argument. They are required to underline the good effects of tourism in the list given and then write their letter.

Activity sheet 3: This sheet is for more able children. They are required to write their own ideas about the good and bad effects of tourism and then write their argument using a selection of suitable phrases.

 ## *Plenary session*

Share the responses to the activity sheets. Are the children agreed they have presented balanced arguments? What conclusions have been drawn?

Follow-up ideas for literacy

+ Challenge the children to find other words and phrases to add to their lists of 'argument words'. They could scan letters to the editors of local or national newspapers to help them in this task.
+ Read some letters to the editor of a local newspaper. Discuss the issues. Challenge the children to send in their own letter.
+ Contact a travel agency to obtain official documents about travelling abroad. Use these to explore official language and its features. Ask the children to write a document about visiting their local area.
+ Find out about working holidays where people are involved in conservation projects. Ask the children

to find more information about these places and the plants and animals that live there.
+ Ask the children to draw and label the 'perfect tourist', for example 'road map so he won't get lost', 'plenty of money in local currency' and 'plastic bag to take rubbish home in'. They could also draw and label the 'worst type of tourist'.

Follow-up ideas for geography

+ Ask the children to plan a holiday to a mountain region. Ask them to mark the route of their journey on a map. Find out how long it will take to get there. They could draw and label the contents of their suitcases to show what clothing and equipment they should take. They could also make up a travel guide for the area by finding out about the local weather, vegetation and wildlife, any precautions people need to take and the best times of the year to visit and why.
+ Use newspaper articles to find out about adverse weather conditions that may affect mountain

regions, for example, avalanches, poor snow in skiing areas, landslides and so on. Discuss how this would affect tourism in the region. How might having fewer tourists affect the local people and the environment? Are weather disasters always a bad thing?

Well, it looks like summer's arrived because I've started to trip over the tourists again in the High St. They park their cars all over the place - not giving a thought to us locals who have to live and work here. Only the other day I was stuck at home all day because some ignorant person had parked his car right across my drive. He didn't return from his mountain trek until late afternoon - boy did I give him a piece of my mind!

What really maddens me, though, is how they drop litter everywhere. You can find bottles and papers all the way up the mountain side. Similarly, the lay-bys and carparks at the base of the mountain paths are equally polluted.

Furthermore, I'm really concerned about the huge numbers of tourists who use the mountains. Many of them don't seem to use the paths - they trample all over the lovely wild flowers and they sometimes get themselves into such predicaments that they end up having to be rescued!

Clearly something needs to be done about these problems. I think we should appoint more people to supervise the area and we should introduce stiffer fines for people who drop litter or park illegally.

Ben Jackson, 68 High St

Oh how I love the tourist season! My bed and breakfast is full of lovely guests, all of whom seem to be really nice people, enjoying the country air that you can only get on a brisk mountain walk! I think they bring so much to our village. They spend money in all the shops, they eat in our tea shops and they make the place seem alive.

On the other hand, I realise that a small minority can spoil it for the rest by their thoughtless behaviour. Yesterday, for example, I discovered that someone had ridden up the mountain path on a motorbike and had caused a great deal of damage to the path. Several sections had collapsed and much of the path had deep ruts in it. This is going to cost our council a lot of money to repair.

Therefore this is why I am writing to agree with the other people who have written in to support the employment of more park rangers.

Marian White, Mountain View Rd

Activity 1

◆ Tourism ◆

◆ Read through the information below. The underlined sentences tell us the good things about tourism in mountainous areas. The sentences that are not underlined tell us the bad things.

Tourists walking in mountains can cause the land to erode.

Tourists can bring in lots of money to an area which helps keep local people in jobs.

Sometimes people get lost or hurt and it can cost a lot of money to rescue them.

Tourists can pollute the area by dropping litter.

Cars bringing people to the area can add to air pollution.

Having tourists in an area can prompt councils to improve roads and other facilities in local towns and villages.

Too many tourists can ruin the peace and beauty of an area.

Sometimes tourists can be involved in conservation projects to help look after the plants and animals in an area.

◆ Choose from the information above to complete the letter to the editor of a newspaper below. Write about the good things first and then the bad things. Then write what YOU think at the end.

To the editor,

I am writing to express my opinion about the good and bad effects of tourists in our area.

Firstly, I want to point out that tourists _____

_____

Furthermore, tourists can _____

_____

On the other hand, I think that tourists can _____

_____

They can also _____

_____

In conclusion I want to say that tourism is _____

_____

Signed

◆ Tourism ◆

◆ Read through the information below. Underline the sentences that tell us the good things about tourism in mountainous areas.

Tourists walking in mountains can cause the land to erode.	Cars bringing people to the area can add to air pollution.
Tourists can bring in lots of money to an area which helps keep local people in jobs.	Having tourists in an area can prompt councils to improve roads and other facilities in local towns and villages.
Sometimes people get lost or hurt and it can cost a lot of money to rescue them.	Too many tourists can ruin the peace and beauty of an area.
Tourists can pollute the area by dropping litter.	Sometimes tourists can be involved in conservation projects to help look after the plants and animals in an area.

◆ Now choose from the information above to complete the letter to the editor of a newspaper below. Write about the good things first and then the bad things. Then write what YOU think at the end.

To the editor,

I am writing to express my opinion about the good and bad effects of tourists in our area.
Firstly,

They also

Furthermore,

On the other hand,

They can also

In conclusion

Signed

◆ Tourism ◆

◆ On the lines below write four sentences about the good effects of tourists in a mountainous region and four sentences about the bad effects.

_____

_____

_____

_____

_____

_____

_____

_____

◆ Now use your sentences to help you write a letter to the editor of a newspaper. Make sure your argument is balanced by writing about both the good and the bad effects of tourism. Write a concluding paragraph. Use some of the phrases from the box below.

furthermore	consequently	as well as
nevertheless	clearly	in contrast
on the other hand	in conclusion	finally
therefore	similarly	as a result

_____

_____

_____

_____

_____

_____

_____

_____

_____

Chapter 9

Rivers – 1

 Literacy objectives

+ To revise the features of explanatory texts, such as the use of impersonal style and technical vocabulary. (Y6: T3, T15)
+ To search for, collect, define and spell technical words. (Y5: T2, W9)

 Geography objectives

(Unit 14)
+ To identify and sequence the components of the water cycle.
+ To know about the water cycle, including condensation and evaporation.
+ To use geographical vocabulary.

 Resources

+ Dictionaries.

 Starting point: Whole class

+ Tell the children that they are going to find out about the water cycle. Ask them to tell you what they can remember about this from their science lessons. Share their ideas and then explain that they will find out if they are right by sharing an information text about it.

 Using the photocopiable text

+ Share an enlarged version of page 54 or provide each pair with a copy.
+ Read the text. How does the information compare with what they had remembered about the water cycle?
+ Explain that the text is an explanatory one because it explains a process. Point out the use of impersonal style and longer, more complex sentences. Explain that explanatory texts also often use difficult technical vocabulary. Underline the following words in the first paragraph: 'environment', 'atmosphere', 'evaporation' and 'precipitation'. Ask the children how important they think it is to understand the meanings of these terms before we can understand the whole paragraph fully.

+ How could they find the meanings of these words? Point out that the text provides us with a meaning for precipitation. Ask the children to remind you how to use a dictionary to find words quickly. Revise alphabetical order (including how to look at the second, third, fourth and so on, letters of a word). Also revise the use of the guide words at the top of the dictionary pages. Ask some children to look up the words and read out the definitions. Discuss the meanings of the terms to ensure the children understand them.
+ Explain that they are now going to use dictionaries to find out the meanings of other words in the text.

 Group activities

Using the differentiated activity sheets

Activity sheet 1: This sheet is aimed at children who need a lot of support in writing dictionary definitions. They are required to match a given term with a definition and write two definitions of their own. They are also asked to write the list out in dictionary order where they need to consider the second letter in the words.

Activity sheet 2: This sheet is aimed at children who can use dictionaries with confidence to find and write definitions. They are also required to order the words up to the fourth letter in the word.

Activity sheet 3: This sheet is for more able children. They are required to find and write definitions for 12 words and then write the words in dictionary order.

Rivers – 1

 Plenary session

✦ Share the responses to the activity sheets. Are they children agreed on the definitions? Go through the dictionary order together – did they remember to look at the 2nd, 3rd and 4th letters of the words, where necessary? How successful were they in learning the words? Do they have any ideas (such as mnemonics) to help them remember the spellings? Discuss the words in relation to the water cycle. Refer to the diagram on page 54 to make sure the children understand where each technical term relates to the cycle. (Cover up the labels on the diagram and ask the children to tell you the technical term for each one before uncovering them to see if they are right.)

 Follow-up ideas for literacy

✦ Challenge the children to re-present the information and diagram about the water cycle for a younger audience. Discuss how to simplify the words used as well as the diagram.

✦ Ask the children to find poems about some of the aspects of the water cycle, for example, the sea, clouds, rivers, lakes and rain. Put the poems on display with a picture of the water cycle as its centrepiece.

✦ Ask the children to design a crossword puzzle using technical words from the water cycle information.

✦ Give the children practice in writing their own explanatory texts by asking them to write about a process they have studied in other subject areas, such as why the Tudors decided to embark on so many voyages of discovery or about the stages of a flowering plant life-cycle.

 Follow-up ideas for geography

✦ Carry out a detailed study of water run-off on the school site. Where does the rain water go? The children could make a note of areas where water collects after heavy rain and map these places. Discuss how these areas could be improved, for example, new downpipes, better drainage and so on.

✦ Visit the local water supplier. How is rainwater collected for public use – are there local reservoirs? Find out how water gets from rivers and reservoirs to our homes. The children could draw and label a flow diagram.

✦ Visit a centre for meteorology. Ask the children to prepare some questions to find out about local rainfall and how it is monitored. For example, what are the wettest and the driest months of the year? How is humidity measured? What types of clouds tell us that it is going to rain? Why don't all clouds release rain? What causes hail?

◆ The water cycle ◆

Water circulates constantly in the environment. Water is continually moving into the atmosphere by evaporation and returning to the earth and sea through precipitation (rain, snow, dew and hail).

The heat of the sun causes water to evaporate from lakes, rivers, oceans, ice and snow, the ground surface, plants (transpiration) and animals (respiration). The water vapour diffuses into the air.

As it rises it cools, causing some of the vapour to form small droplets of water or ice crystals (condensation), which become visible as clouds. When the particles join together to form larger droplets, they fall back to earth as rain or snow.

Rain falling onto the earth is partly absorbed into the ground and partly runs off into streams and rivers which make their way to the sea.

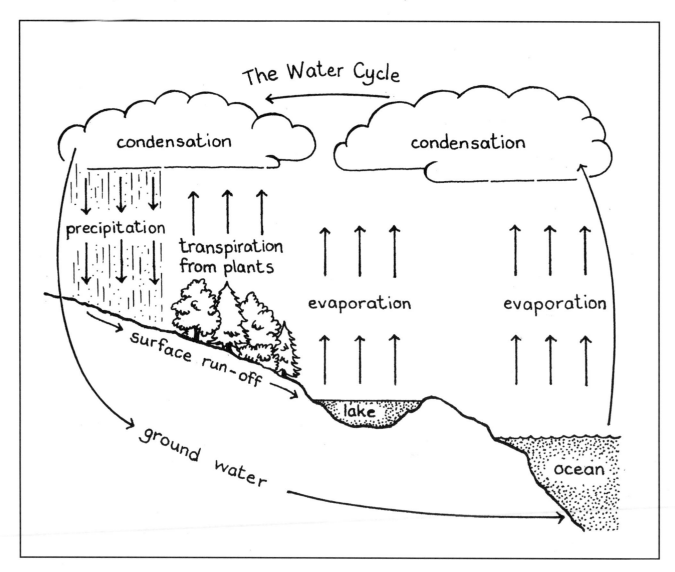

✦ The water cycle ✦

✦ Use a dictionary to help you match the words below to their correct definitions. Write in the definitions that are missing.

condensation	small particles of water in the air (gas)
atmosphere	when liquids change to a gas
evaporation	
surface	when vapour changes to a liquid
droplet	a very small piece
particle	
vapour	a small drop
cycle	the gases surrounding the earth

✦ Now write out the list of words in dictionary order. The first and last have been done for you.

1. atmosphere 2. _____ 3. _____

4. _____ 5. _____ 6. _____

7. _____   8. vapour

✦ Choose three of the words and try to learn how to spell them. Look carefully at each word, say it, write it down, look carefully again and then cover up the word and try to write it.

©Hopscotch Educational Publishing

Name _____

◆ The water cycle ◆

◆ Use a dictionary to help you write a definition for each of the words below.

condensation	
atmosphere	
evaporation	
visible	
continual	
particle	
vapour	
environment	

◆ Now write the words in dictionary order.

1. _____	4. _____	7. _____
2. _____	5. _____	8. _____
3. _____	6. _____	

◆ Choose four of the words and try to learn how to spell them. Look carefully at each word, say it, write it down, look carefully again and then cover up the word and try to write it.

©Hopscotch Educational Publishing

✦ The water cycle ✦

✦ Use a dictionary to help you write a definition for each of the words below.

transpiration	evaporation	condensation	environment
atmosphere	vapour	respiration	continual
precipitation	crystal	surface	circulate

_____

_____

_____

_____

_____

_____

_____

_____

_____

_____

_____

_____

✦ Now write the words in dictionary order.

1. _____ 7. _____

2. _____ 8. _____

3. _____ 9. _____

4. _____ 10. _____

5. _____ 11. _____

6. _____ 12. _____

✦ Choose six of the words and try to learn how to spell them. Look carefully
at each word, say it, write it down, look carefully again and then cover up
the word and try to write it.

©Hopscotch Educational Publishing

Rivers – 2

Literacy objectives

✦ To divide whole texts into paragraphs, paying attention to the sequence of paragraphs and to the links between one paragraph and the next through the use of connectives. (Y6: T3, T21)

Geography objectives

(Unit 14)
✦ To understand how rivers affect the landscape.
✦ To understand how and why a river changes.
✦ To know how rivers erode, transport and deposit materials producing particular landscape features.
✦ To use geographical vocabulary.

Resources

✦ Pictures of river landscapes to show, for example, meanders, river valleys, estuaries, deltas, river banks and so on.
✦ Maps showing location of local, UK and foreign rivers.
✦ Information books on rivers that show the text presented in paragraphs.

Starting point: Whole class

✦ Tell the children that they are going to find out about rivers. Ask them to tell you the names of any rivers they have heard of – locally, nationally or worldwide. Write the names of the rivers on the board. Use maps to locate some of them to show their position in relation to the local area.
✦ Ask the children to tell you what they already know about rivers. Do they know what they can be used for, for example? Have they ever travelled on a river?
✦ Tell them that they are now going to read about how rivers are formed and what happens to them as they move along.

Using the photocopiable text

✦ Enlarge the text on page 60 or arrange for each pair of children to have a copy.
✦ Share the text. Discuss any unfamiliar words. Use the pictures to illustrate the content of the text as you reread it for understanding. Had the children ever thought before about how rivers are formed or where they travel to? Were they aware of how water could wear away the land in this way? Have they ever seen meanders in real rivers or stood at a place where a river meets the sea? Share their ideas and experiences.
✦ Ask them to look at the text again and tell you what they notice about the way it is set out. Open one of the information books to compare how the text inside is set out in paragraphs. Talk about the reasons for using paragraphs. How do they help us with reading? How do we decide when to begin a new paragraph when we are writing?
✦ Explain that you want them to divide the text on page 60 into paragraphs. Show them where the first paragraph ends (the sentence beginning 'This water...' and ending with '...which drain water from the areas of high land.') Explain that the first paragraph describes how water falling on high land runs off the land to form streams. Cut out the paragraph and place it on the board using Blu-tac.
✦ Circle the word 'As' at the beginning of the next paragraph. Remind the children that this is a connective – it is used to make a link between the end of the first paragraph and the beginning of the next. Can they work out where this second paragraph ends? Agree that the second paragraph tells us how a river is formed.
✦ Agree the third, fourth and last paragraphs together, looking at the different connectives used. Look at the layout of the cut out paragraphs. Does it make it much easier to read? Would this help us to find specific information more quickly now? Discuss the importance of the correct sequencing of the paragraphs – how they tell us about the stages of river development from the beginning to the end and how it would not make sense to order them in a different way.
✦ Explain to the children that they are now going to divide another text into paragraphs in the same way.

Rivers – 2

 Group activities

Using the differentiated activity sheets

Activity sheet 1: This sheet is aimed at children who need a lot of support in deciding where paragraphs should be. They are given help with the first one. The text is easier than on the other sheets.

Activity sheet 2: This sheet is aimed at children who are more confident in deciding where paragraphs should go. The text is more complex.

Activity sheet 3: This sheet is for more able children. The text is longer and more complex.

 Plenary session

✦ Share the responses to the activity sheets. Are the children agreed where the paragraphs should go? Are they pleased with the way they presented their final work? How could it be improved – more illustrations? A border? What else have they learned about how rivers can change the landscape? Can they explain what a meander is? A waterfall?

 Follow-up ideas for literacy

✦ The children could use information books, CD-Roms and the Internet to find out about a well-known river. They could produce an information leaflet using a desktop publishing program on the computer.

✦ Share some poems about rivers, such as 'The Cataract of Lodore' by Robert Southey (*The New Oxford Treasury of Children's Poems*, OUP) or 'A River's Story' by Raymond Wilson (*Earthways, Earthwise, Poems on Conservation*, selected by Judith Nicholls, OUP).

✦ Have some fun making up ways to remember how to spell some of the technical terms for rivers, for example:

me and 'er = meander

every river overflows sometimes in our neighbourhood = **e r o s i o n**

 Follow-up ideas for geography

✦ Visit a local stream or river. Ask the children to sketch it and label the features. Take photographs of features such as meanders. Measure the rate of flow on the inside and outside of bends. Can the children see any signs of pollution? Is the river flowing freely? Back at school make a large mural of the river. Ask the children to label it with descriptions of each feature and any observations they noted. They could make comparisons between their river and another one in a different location.

✦ Go on a boat trip up a river such as the Thames. Ask the children to look out for jobs and activities associated with the river such as barges, pleasure boats, restaurants, river police and so on. Find out more about these jobs and how important the river is to them.

✦ Ask the children to make an information book about a selected river. Ask them to include maps showing its location, diagrams showing special features and information gathered from newspapers, books, CD-Roms and the Internet.

River formation

When snow, sleet or rain fall on the earth, a lot of the water is stored in some way. Some of it soaks into the surface and is stored underground. Some of it is stored as snowcaps on high mountains and some is stored in lakes or the sea. When rain falls on hills and mountains, some of it runs down the surface as 'run-off'. This water, together with water that seeps out of the ground and water from snowcaps that have melted, runs off the land and collects in little streams which drain water from the areas of high land. As the streams move down the hills and mountains, they collect more water along the way. Several streams join up with each other and gradually the streams get bigger and bigger because they are carrying more water. Eventually they turn into rivers. As the river moves down the steep slopes, it gets faster and faster. The movement of the water causes the river to dislodge rocks, boulders and soil as it goes. This material, called 'debris', rubs against the river bed and banks, wearing the land away. This is called 'erosion'. When the river meets the flat plains below the mountains and hills, the water movement slows down. The river starts to drop (or 'deposit') the large rocks and boulders it was carrying but it still carries smaller particles and soil. Because the river is not as strong now that it is moving more slowly, it does not wear away the land as much. When the river comes to areas of land that are made of hard rock, the river cannot erode the land so it bends around it instead. These bends in the river are called 'meanders'. Finally, most rivers end up flowing into seas. The river slows down even more now and sometimes it deposits all the soil and small particles it was carrying at its mouth. This sometimes causes a large swampy plain to form, known as a 'delta'.

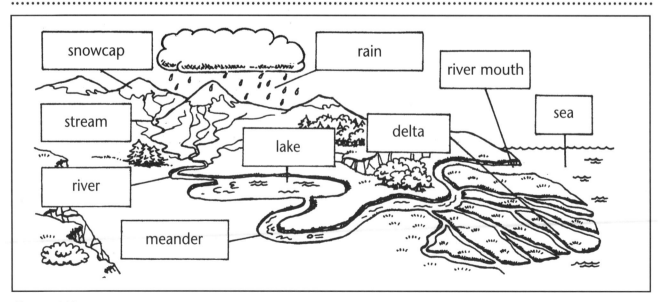

Photocopiable

©Hopscotch Educational Publishing

✦ Rivers ✦

✦ Read through the information below. Divide it into three paragraphs. The end of the first paragraph has been marked for you. Decide where the third one should start. Then cut out the paragraphs and the three pictures. Glue them on to another sheet of paper in the correct order.

When rains falls on to hills and mountains, some of it soaks into the ground and some of it runs off along the surface. Because the ground is steep, this water moves very quickly down the slope, forming little streams. The little streams join up to make a big <u>river.</u> As the river moves down the slope it wears away the rocks. In some places, waterfalls can be made. This happens when soft rock lies near hard rock. The hard rock doesn't wear away but the soft rock does so the water eats into the soft rock, making a hole. Over time the hole gets deeper and deeper, making the water fall further and further. Once the river meets flatter land, it slows down. The river doesn't wear away the rocks so much any more because the water is moving more slowly. So when it comes to some hard rock, it bends around it instead of wearing it away. These bends are called 'meanders'.

◆ R i v e r s ◆

✦ Read through the information below. Divide it into three paragraphs. Cut out the three paragraphs and the three illustrations and glue them on to another sheet of paper in the correct sequence. Write a suitable heading.

Most rivers begin on the steeper slopes of hills and mountains. The steeper the slope, the faster the river flows and the harder it eats into the rocks. These rocks can be either hard or soft. Hard rocks wear down more slowly than softer rocks. Where a river flows over first a hard area of rock, then a soft area, it eats away at the soft rock, making a hole. The hard rock forms a ledge and as the water flows over the ledge, it forms a waterfall. When the river flows across flatter land, it slows down. Instead of moving quickly over hard rock areas, it now bends around them. These bends are called 'meanders'. Sometimes a meander forms a very deep curve and instead of flowing all the way round, the river finds a short cut and the old meander is left as a semicircular lake (called an 'ox-bow lake'). Finally, when the river meets the sea, it slows down further. It drops ('deposits') even more of the soil it is carrying to form a fan-shaped area called an 'alluvial fan'.

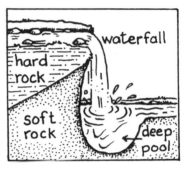

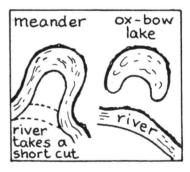

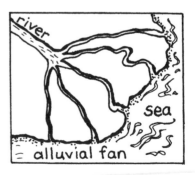

✦ Rivers ✦

✦ Read through the information below. Divide it into three paragraphs. Cut out the three paragraphs and the three illustrations and glue them on to another sheet of paper in the correct sequence. Write a suitable heading.

Most rivers begin on the steeper slopes of hills and mountains. The steeper the slope, the faster the river flows and the harder it cuts into the rocks. These rocks can wear down at different rates. Hard rocks are worn down more slowly than softer rocks. Where a river flows over first a hard rock area, then a soft rock area, it forms a ledge and creates a waterfall. As the softer rock is worn away and the water has to fall further, it pounds the rocks harder and often a deep pool develops at the base of the waterfall. When the river flows across flatter land, it slows down. Instead of rushing over obstacles it now flows around them. When water flows around a bend (a 'meander'), the water on the outside of the bend has to flow further than the water on the inside, so it flows faster. This causes the river to cut away or 'erode' the outside of the bends more quickly. The water on the inside of the bend flows more slowly and therefore begins to drop some of the rocks and soil it is carrying. Sometimes a meander develops such a curve that the banks on one side are cut back into the banks on the other side. The river finds a short cut and the old meander is left as a semicircular lake (called an 'ox-bow lake'). Finally, when the river meets the sea, it slows down further. It drops ('deposits') even more of the soil it is carrying to form a fan-shaped area called an 'alluvial fan'. 'Deltas' form at some river mouths where big banks of deposits can form far out into the sea.

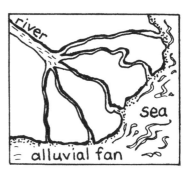